CHARACTER
UNDER
CONSTRUCTION

Nancy Van Pelt

First published 2009

© 2009

British Library Cataloguing in Publication Data. A catalogue record for this book is available from the British Library.

ISBN 978-1-906381-48-6

Published by Autumn House, Grantham, Lincolnshire.

Printed in Thailand.

Bible versions used, indicated by initials:
The Message: The Bible in Contemporary Language, Eugene H. Peterson (NavPress) – MGE
New King James Version (Thomas Nelson) – NKJV
The New Testament in Modern English by J. B. Phillips (Collins) – JBP
King James Version – KJV

What is character?

Character refers to moral excellence.

It involves honesty, self-control, thoughtfulness of others, religious loyalty, moral ideals, conscience and the ability to inhibit impulses.

It is the *mark* of a person – the pattern of traits upon his lifestyle.

An inscription?

The word *character* comes from the Greek word meaning engrave.

Instruction in youth is like engraving in stone.
Columbian proverb

What kind of permanent inscription is now being deeply etched into the very heart and soul of your child?

Nature or nurture?

A newborn baby does not possess character. However, an infant has potential or the raw materials for character development. Thus, active character development begins at birth.

All the attitudes and facets that go into shaping a child's character are *learned*.

It's your responsibility!

The child that's left to himself will put his mother to shame.
Gaelic proverb

The responsibility of character development rests squarely on the parents' shoulders.

Cop-outs such as 'bad genes' won't hold up.

Don't expect instant results

Because the results of building character do not appear immediately (many parents define the results solely in terms of whether a child obeys or not) parents frequently neglect (or carry out inconsistently or haphazardly) the task of character development.

But it is the long-term *value*, not the *immediacy* of the results that should be stressed.

Begin at the beginning

During the early years of life, character development is most rapid and inherently most susceptible to guidance.

Let every Christian father and mother realise that when their child is 3 years old they have already done more than half of all they will ever do for his character.

Catch them young

The first five or six years are
the most formative period.

Every parent can rest assured
that the beginnings of character
development are being laid
and that a multitude of
influences are already at
work during infancy.

Early lessons stick

The attitudes a child learns during the first five to seven years of his life become almost permanent. When the opportunities of these early years are missed, they are gone forever.

If parents want a child to be obedient, kind, honest, faithful, unselfish, patient and God-fearing, they should make these characteristics the conscious objective of their early teaching.

Set a good example in the home

The atmosphere of the home is particularly important to the child's budding development.

If the parents do not respect each other, if they quarrel all the time or are jealous or untruthful, if they engage in power struggles of any kind, their child will suffer some distortion of development – regardless of how carefully they try to hide their own problems.

Watch your own behaviour

The main ingredient for a child's character development is that the parents relate to each other with mutual love, respect and appreciation.

As surely as a mirror, the child will reflect the same character traits to which it is continually exposed.

Accentuate
the positive

Repeated verdicts about being 'bad' or 'good' will directly influence his character.

All indications of your child's standard of behaviour are nurtured by repeated positive reinforcement.

When he accomplishes any task, reinforce your child's good behaviour and ignore any negative aspects, commenting only on what was done correctly.

Learning right from wrong takes time

No child will develop the ability to choose between right and wrong by himself.

He must be taught these standards through a long, slow process that extends from infancy well into adolescence.

Impose restrictions

Since a young child is incapable of controlling his own conduct, his behaviour must be controlled through restrictions.

These restrictions are first imposed by the family and later by the school, church and society.

The lesson of love

Parents should teach a child
to love them so that in turn he
will learn how to love others.

Gradually they should teach
a child that by breaking rules
he hurts others.

Inner controls

Before a youngster leaves childhood he is expected to have developed inner controls that will help him make proper choices.

As the child grows, the parents should gradually shift away from heavy external controls so that the child can develop internal controls.

The ultimate goal

By the time the youngster reaches adolescence, he should be able to control much of his own conduct.

By the time he reaches legal maturity, the transition should be complete.

A matter of conscience

When a child learns to love and respect the rights and privileges of others, he will feel anxious or guilty when he hurts others.

Such feelings mark the beginnings of a tender conscience.

How conscience develops

The young child learns that certain acts are not acceptable because when one does them a sure and certain punishment follows.

Anxiety then follows the punishment.

In order to reduce anxiety the child learns not to repeat the behaviour.

Conscience as a guide to conduct

Once the conscience has been developed, it can be used as a guide for conduct. If a child's conduct does not measure up to the standard, he will be likely to feel guilty and ashamed.

Guilt is the negative feeling experienced when one does not live up to the previously taught standard of conformity.

When a child feels guilty, he realises that his behaviour has fallen below the standard he has set for himself.

Carefully does it!

It is important during this process that parents do not teach their child to fear only the suffering that his improper behaviour brings through punishment.

Such fear takes away his ability to appreciate the consequences his actions have on others.

Firm but affectionate parents carefully take the time to explain the consequences of behaviour.

Developing self-control

We do not want our children to form right habits only because they fear punishment.

We want them to develop internal controls so that when Mummy or Daddy is not present, even when punishment will not be the end result, the child will still choose a proper course of action.

The benefits of self-control

Self-control will permit the child to choose thoughtfully the act he wishes to accomplish.

A multiplicity of rational and irrational choices may surround the child, but if he is being guided by budding inner controls, he will not yield to his own personal interests.

He will not act only from impulse but will deliberate and choose wisely.

Be realistic

As parents we must not expect too much too soon from a child.

One foolish act of a child does not make him a criminal.

However, unless a child develops self-control, he will be constantly yielding to the wishes of others.

Be patient

It takes several years before a child has the capability of learning and comprehending the principles of right and wrong.

Parents sometimes forget the gradual process by which character is formed.

Because they have taught a child once, they expect him to remember forever.

It takes time

It is through trial and error that a child learns right from wrong.

Year by year, as he matures and experiences the natural consequences of his behaviour, he will gradually learn to make proper choices.

Broadening horizons

Children initially learn right from wrong from parents, brothers and sisters, and other family members.

When they get older, their social horizons broaden to include their neighbours, school and church friends.

Now the child becomes aware that the standards held within the home are not always held by others.

Peer pressure

As the opportunity for a child to interact within a social circle increases, so does peer influence.

When home standards conflict with peer standards, peer pressure will almost always win out.

If a child lacks the ability to decide for himself, his choices will be almost entirely impulsive or dependent on what his peer group urges.

Guide him to choose his friends wisely

Since peer pressure strongly affects a child's character development, it is important that the group with which he identifies has moral standards that conform to those taught in the home.

The *type* of friends a child has is much more important than the *number* of friends he enjoys.

Keep things
in perspective

One isolated incident does
not ruin character.

Naturally, such behaviour
concerns you, but you must
realise that it is the *repetition*
of a particular behaviour
pattern that makes a habit
and forms character.

Patterns of behaviour

Every time a child is allowed to misbehave, it establishes a habit pattern that lays a potential hazard to character development.

Conversely, every time a child repeats a positive course of action, character is being built.

One thing
leads to another

Thoughts form actions.
Actions form habits.
Habits form character.
Sow character and you
  reap destiny.

Reward good behaviour

Parental guidance succeeds the best when the child can associate pleasant reactions with what is right and unpleasant reactions with what is wrong.

For example, a child will learn to repeat acts for which he is rewarded.

It has been reliably established that reward is a powerful determinant of good behaviour.

Bribery?

Some adults ignore the techniques of positive reinforcement because they misconstrue it as bribery.

Rewards make personal effort worthwhile, yet parents fail to use them where they do the most good – with their child.

Reinforcers and punishers

Research on behaviour has convincingly demonstrated that the consequences that *follow* a behaviour will strengthen or weaken that behaviour.

Those that strengthen a particular behaviour are called *reinforcers;* those that weaken a behaviour are called *punishers*.

The law of reinforcement

The most effective technique for controlling behaviour co-operates with the law of reinforcement: Behaviour that achieves desired consequences will recur.

Simply stated, if a child likes what happens as a result of his behaviour, he will be inclined to repeat it.

Token reinforcers – a quick fix?

Such things as points, stars, stamps, charts and money fall into the realm of token reinforcers.

The child accumulates these tokens and exchanges them for a long-range goal.

Using this method can help parents effect the greatest possible change in the least amount of time.

How it works

Draw up a list of responsibilities or behaviours that need reinforcing. Ten to fifteen is sufficient for most children – fewer for a small child and more for an older child.

Include on the list some things the child already does well in order to make it encouraging to earn points.

Rewards to use

The child should place stamps, points, stars or coloured ticks beside each item completed satisfactorily. Weight the most difficult tasks with the most points.

An alternative method is to give a small sum of money for each item done properly.

You can also deduct points or money for poor or negligent behaviour.

Keep up the interest

You might ask your child to draw or paste a picture of the payoff on the chart to help him visualise the goal.

At the end of each week add up the points or stars or money so the child can see his progress.

You need to give him encouragement and incentive to keep going.

Cultivate a new habit

The list of behaviours should not change for four to six weeks, since it generally takes that amount of time to establish a new habit.

Charts must be adapted to the age of the child, but are effective for children as young as 3 right through the teen years.

Variation on the theme

Another variation to the point programme is the grab bag.

You will need to purchase inexpensive objects from the toyshop and fill a bag with them.

When a child performs the appropriate behaviour, allow him to reach into the bag and take out one object.

Ignore negative behaviour

As you work to improve your child's behaviour, pay little or no attention to what the child does that you do not want him to do.

There are tangible benefits in reinforcing the good behaviour and overlooking the bad.

Counterproductive?

Ignore the behaviour you wish to extinguish.

Negative comments about it may only reinforce it!

Learn to reward positive behaviour, and the unreinforced behaviour will eventually disappear.

No mixed messages

Both parents should participate in the programme in order for the process to move rapidly.

Both parents should discuss the type of reinforcement programme used, and they should agree ahead of time concerning what reinforcers and punishers will work best.

Catch them red-handed!

A good motto for parents might be: *Catch your child being good, and reward him for it.*

Stop acting as though you were trying to catch your youngster doing something wrong so that you can shout at him.

Instead, look for good behaviour that you can reinforce with positive comments.

Give them

responsibility

The assumption of responsibility
should be pleasurable, for it produces
a feeling of satisfaction and fulfilment.

It makes a person feel
important and useful.

These good feelings are a reward in
themselves, and they provide a solid
foundation for developing self-respect.

Make work fun

A child can enjoy doing necessary tasks and doing them well if, when he is between the ages of 2 and 7, he learns to accept work as a part of living.

But you should make work fun for him.

If a child shows signs of boredom, give him a new task that offers a challenge.

Make it a game

Make a list of jobs, each on a separate piece of paper, and drop them all in a bag. Have each child draw a job from inside the bag. 'You draw your job and you take your chances!'

Put on favourite music and whistle or sing while you work.

Play 'Beat the clock' by racing against time.

Make it a family affair

A child works better if someone
works along with him.

The family can go outside and work
together in the garden, each one
having a different task but all working
together.

This can be a real togetherness time,
an opportunity for communicating,
teaching, sharing and playing.

The value of work

Work is the best discipline a child can have, but it should not be used as a punishment.

Parents should impress on their child's mind that work is noble and an essential part of developing a healthy mind and body.

The devil finds work . . .

If the active minds and hands of youth are not directed to useful tasks, they will find mischief to do which may permanently injure character development.

Channel their energy into useful activities.

Assault and battery on character?

Any activity that absorbs a large portion of a child's time will influence his character.

Since the average child watches nearly three hours of television daily, it exerts a major influence on his character.

Some researchers actually feel that television is a 'school of violence' which teaches young people that crime is not reprehensible, but a great adventure.

Watch what they're watching!

Researchers have found that much of what a child sees on the screen he will carry over into his day-by-day play.

A young child is particularly susceptible to such influences because he cannot differentiate between fantasy and reality as well as older children and adults can.

Lessons in mediocrity

Television also frequently advocates mediocre (and in some cases less than mediocre) values.

Many shows that are considered good family entertainment depict many questionable, even immoral, values.

Every time a child views such things, it makes an impression on his mind which, when repeated, will determine a habit, and habits determine character.

UNDER
CONSTRUCTION

A communication killer

In addition, TV can cut family communication, offer a child a convenient crutch so that he can withdraw from family interaction, produce callousness towards human suffering, and consume a large share of leisure time, thus reducing play activity.

A daily diet?

Regardless of how you feel about television, it is unconsciously shaping your child's character (as well as yours).

We need to develop self-control and parental control so that TV, video games and DVDs do not constitute a steady daily diet.

More danger zones

Other forms of entertainment are just as destined to destroy elements of character within a child.

These things include various movies, books, magazines, forms of music, places of amusement and the Internet.

The solution does not lie in mere banishment of these items, but in providing adequate substitutes.

Monitor your child's Internet use

Parents can be very naive about what their child is seeing, as well as how easy this is to access. Any child who regularly surfs the Web will stumble onto the hard-core stuff sooner or later.

Porn poses a real threat to children, especially boys.

Just one exposure can set the stage for addiction in some boys that will hold them captive for life.

Internet predators

The Internet holds special dangers because predators quickly take advantage of Web anonymity to build online relationships with the naive and inexperienced.

The vast majority of predators routinely scan chat rooms, instant messaging, email or discussion boards to establish contact.

Many pre-teens and teens use online peer support to deal with their problems. Predators go to such online areas to search for vulnerable candidates.

The most vulnerable age

Young adolescents are the most vulnerable since they are exploring their sexuality, are moving away from parental control and looking for new relationships outside the family.

They are most likely to take uncalculated risks without understanding the implications.

What to look out for

Characteristics of those most vulnerable might include: new to online activity, become aggressive computer users, apt to try risky activities, actively seeking attention or affection, rebellious, isolated or lonely, curious, exhibit confused sexual identity, or are attracted by subcultures.

Parents beware: *Kids think they know the dangers on the Internet while they remain quite naive.*

It's good to talk

Talk openly about Internet safety with the whole family. Make it a topic for supper conversation.

Remind all family members that safeguarding values is a priority in your home.

Discuss what King David means when he says in Psalms 101:3: 'I will set no wicked thing before mine eyes.' (KJV.)

Spiritual training

If parents want a child to be obedient, kind, honest, faithful, unselfish, patient and God-fearing, they should make these characteristics the conscious objective of their early teaching.

Between 1 and 7 years of age, a youngster is most susceptible to religious training. His concept of right and wrong is formed during this time, and his ideas of God take shape.

Don't wait
until it's too late!

Depriving a child of spiritual
training, or subjecting him
to the misapplication of it,
severely limits his capacity
ever to reach spiritual maturity.

When parents say that they will
wait until their child is old enough to
decide for himself if he wants religion,
they have almost guaranteed that he
will decide against it.

Remember you are being watched!

Live out consistent Christian behaviour. Your child's everyday experiences of life will influence his religious experience.

If you wish your child to incorporate spiritual values into his life, you must first exemplify them in your own.

Prioritise!

A person makes time for that which means the most to him.

Think it through. Does God take top priority in your life?

Then, and only then, will your youngster give him first place in his life.

Family worship

Set up a regular time for family devotions and make no exceptions unless absolutely necessary.

Read a passage of Scripture. Make the Bible interesting to your child.

There is also a place for music.

Have prayer together, allowing each child to join in.

Two essentials

Two things are essential to character development:

1. The admirable qualities that formulate character, and

2. A strong sense of self-respect, which will enable a person to control his conduct.

Self-respect is vital

A child may have many admirable traits, but if he has no self-respect, he will have little desire to display his admirable qualities or may do so only sporadically.

So it is *self-respect* that is the determining factor in character development.

A common complaint

Nearly everyone suffers
from feelings of inadequacy.

We see evidence of this mass
tragedy on every hand – in every
neighbourhood, church and school.

Although feelings of inadequacy
are evident in small children, it
becomes particularly apparent during
adolescence. Most teenagers are
bitterly disappointed in who they
are, what they look like, and what
they are accomplishing.

The reason?

Why do so many people grow up
disliking themselves? How are the
opinions of self formed? What makes
a child think about himself the way
he does?

It all begins in the tender years of childhood.

Parents have not understood how to
structure the child's environment so
that self-respect can be built instead
of destroyed.

A killer disease?

Heart disease is the greatest killer disease in the Western world.

However, a lack of self-respect plagues more people, cripples more lives, and renders useless more individuals than the world's greatest health problem.

What is self-respect?

It is the mental picture of oneself formed by feedback accumulated from others over the years and through the experiences of life.

Those who possess it will function well rather than stumble and grope through life.

The results of healthy self-respect

People who possess self-respect like themselves, have confidence in their abilities, and are satisfied with their life and work.

Since they have confidence in their abilities, they are able to risk attempting new things.

If they encounter failures, they have the ability to deal with them without whipping themselves mercilessly with guilt. They can move out of a failure pattern and begin anew.

When you are conscious of your worth . . .

Those with self-respect not only feel innate value, but they also know they have an important contribution to make in life.

They feel loved and, therefore, can genuinely love others.

Because they feel good about themselves, they are able to respond positively to people and life situations.

You feel comfortable with yourself

These people are free to throw their energies into solving problems rather than fainting under their weight.

They can accept the value of their accomplishments without being conceited.

Consequently, they feel equal to others and able to measure up to others' positive opinions of them.

What it's not

Self-respect is not 'self-love' in an egotistical, prideful sense.

In fact, bragging and boasting about oneself and one's accomplishments are classic symptoms of low self-worth.

Self-respect is vital to success

How your child feels about himself will determine his success or failure in each of life's endeavours.

How he perceives himself will influence his behaviour and his grades – also his choice of male and female friends, schools and career.

His view of himself, in short, influences every decision he will ever make.

Be warned!

Every word, action and method of child-training you now employ either builds or destroys your child's self-image.

So be careful!

It's not down to what you can do

Self-respect cannot be measured through talent or capabilities.

Many people who possess tremendous talent and ability may still have a crippling self-concept.

Where do negative feelings originate?

It all begins in the tender years of childhood.

Subjected to a constant barrage of put-downs, along with non-verbal disrespect or emotional neglect, a child begins to grow up feeling ashamed of and dissatisfied with himself.

The seeds for thoughts such as 'I'm no good' or 'I can never measure up to what my parents want from me' begin to sprout.

Society's fault as well?

The structure of society is designed to promote such feelings. They begin in the formative years and are nurtured by a performance-oriented society.

Competition to be the best permeates every classroom.

Awards and rewards go to the winners of sports and other activities.

Winners and losers

Wherever there are winners,
there must also be losers.

Those who play the game
and lose feel the pains of
unacceptance and inferiority.

Give support

Parents fail to render the support needed for feelings of adequacy to develop during the tender years.

Belittling remarks at home, added to the competition-packed society, set the stage for a child to belittle and refuse to accept himself.

This has the potential of initiating a lifetime of self-castigation, self-recrimination and self-unacceptability.

Fragile! Handle with care!

By the time the child blows out that one little candle on his first birthday cake, his self-respect is already vulnerable.

When an infant is only a few months old, he can distinguish between censure and praise.

His awareness of the love and respect of his parents lays the crucial foundation for his own self-respect.

Self-respect is learned

A child is not born feeling good about himself, although tendencies towards either positive or negative feelings about oneself may be inherent. Self-respect generally evolves from a child's daily interactions with others.

The more positive experiences you provide for your child and the more positive feedback he receives from you, then the greater the chances that he will *learn* that he is a person of worth and adequacy.

UNDER CONSTRUCTION

Self-respect
must be earned

A worthwhile task well done will foster feelings of adequacy. Spoken or unspoken, 'How am I doing?' lurks in every child's subconscious mind.

A child could never like himself if he thought that he couldn't do anything well.

By developing skills and abilities a child can enhance his sense of adequacy.

Self-respect must be experienced

Loving your child is not enough.

Your child must *feel* your acceptance of him as a person – *feel* your appreciation of his individual worth, whether or not he accomplishes anything great in life.

The greatest gift

Love is not the greatest gift parents can give to a child.

Self-respect is.

A child is not capable of experiencing or returning love until he first learns to respect himself.

Three feelings . . .

Three feelings that a child senses significantly affect his comprehension of self-worth: *uniqueness, belonging and human love.*

These three feelings combine to give stability and support to the structure of the self-concept.

Uniqueness

Every person is unique, and the specialness of a child deserves respect.

This uniqueness can be found by being the oldest, middle or youngest child, or through a special talent or ability.

Recognise in each of your children the uniqueness he brings to your family, and feel that he can fill an important spot in your life.

Belonging

A child senses whether he 'belongs' in the family.

The child who feels that he is an unnecessary appendage or believes that he is a 'fifth wheel' or an 'unhappy accident' will have a difficult time feeling respected.

Human love

Love is defined here as a valuing of
your child, a tender caring. It means
that your youngster remains special
and dear to you even if you don't
approve of all he does.

We all know that children need
love, but many of us assume that
our children automatically know
that we love them.

A child needs to be certain
he is loved.

No conditions!

Innocently, sometimes, parents convey to a child that he is not loved or cared for.

'If you are a good girl, Mummy will love you. If you aren't a good girl, Mummy can't love you.'

This makes love conditional on good behaviour.

Love without limits

Love your child because he is yours.

You must love little Johnny, not because he is behaving right now, not because he gets good marks in school, not because he excels in sports, not because he is an obedient child, but because he is yours.

You love him because he is Johnny.

The value of unconditional love

When you love your child in this manner, he will sense that he belongs, that he is needed, and that he is respected, and these inner feelings of security will help him grow up into a sound, mature person.

Society's false value

One of the ways by which society measures the worth of an individual is his innate intelligence.

Parents of slow learners should de-emphasise the importance of academic excellence and focus instead on the child's strengths and good qualities.

In the light of eternity, there are more important things in life than school reports with straight A's!

A potential downward spiral?

The child who lacks average mental ability may find himself caught in a whirlpool of depression – the wasted victim of another false value created by our society.

The worth of an individual must not be measured by his IQ!

Develop a
special talent

Parents should help this child develop
a special talent that will compensate
for his weaknesses.

Slow learners are often good with their
hands.

Wise parents will help him find a skill
he enjoys and provide the opportunity
for him to master it.

Developing a special skill will give your
child a sense of worth.

Not enough?

People often naively assert that all a child needs is love and he will develop satisfactorily.

No! Love is not enough.

You may be able to control factors inside the home, but you cannot control the world outside your home.

Your child must be able to function adequately in spite of the problems life has dealt him.

Teach him to cope, not mope

Our job as parents is not to protect our children from every hurt in life, but rather to prepare our children to accept the inevitable hurts and nobly rise above them.

In other words, we can teach our children to cope with the false values that stem from society.

It's important to teach them to grow emotionally through problems!

Laugh!

Your example will mean a lot.

If you can laugh at your own shortcomings and mistakes, this will go a long way in helping your child over some of the rough spots of life.

Teach your child to remember his failures with a smile.

Self-depreciation is a no-no

Let your child know you will not allow him to depreciate himself or anyone else.

Begin this policy early in life and enforce it.

However, if you belittle yourself, the entire concept will crumble.

Be careful with words

A critical parent arouses in his child feelings of rejection.

Yelling, screaming and constant criticism tell a child that you do not love him or care about his feelings.

'Watch the way you talk. . . .
Say only what helps,
each word a gift.'
Ephesians 4:29, MGE.

Show your appreciation

Feelings of unacceptance do not always have to be verbalised to be experienced.

A lack of appreciation or recognition speaks as loudly as if it were verbally announced.

Whether spoken or unspoken, criticism is by far the most common and destructive cause of low self-esteem.

Guilty as charged?

If you haven't shown acceptance towards your child, first admit it and then ask God's forgiveness.

Recognise that your child is a special gift to you and that God has a special purpose for him.

Don't be
a bossy boots!

An adult's domineering or bossy
attitude implies to the child that
he isn't capable of completing an
assigned task unless his parent is
there to supervise.

Authoritarian parents weaken self-
worth. A child who is constantly told
what to do develops few inner controls
and lacks faith in his own abilities to
carry out tasks by himself.

A child needs training and guidance,
but not in an overbearing manner.

Mother, but don't smother

Over-protectiveness or excessive sheltering can also make a child feel rejected because he never has an opportunity to make decisions for himself.

A mother who fights all the neighbourhood battles in order to protect her 'precious' from the cruel world inhibits his progress towards a positive self-image.

Quality time

Parents are advised to spend more time with a child, yet it is not quantity but quality time that is important.

Nothing spells love to a child more than your personal, patient interest in his thoughts and questions.

Keep on loving

We love our children deeply, we care for them, we'd even give our lives for them.

And yet in the day-to-day struggle for existence, some of our love gets lost.

Our divine Example

The key is the ability to accept the child at all times, while perhaps not accepting everything he does.

Just as God hates sin but loves the sinner, so parents should differentiate between the child's behaviour and the child himself if they want him to build a positive self-image.

Always show acceptance

The more acceptance he finds from his family, the more rejection he can withstand from outside.

Thus, although parents are not totally responsible for a child's self-concept, they play a major role, because how they relate to their child during the early years at home sets the stage for his later success or failure.

A cry for help?

The worse a child's behaviour, the greater his cry for approval.

The more your child misbehaves – the more withdrawn or obnoxious he is – the more starved he is for attention and acceptance.

The greater the defences, the withdrawal or misbehaviour, the greater the need.

Self-concepts can change

A child's self-concept is not forged for all time, although once established it is not easily disturbed.

Since feelings of worth are learned, earned and experienced rather than inherited, attitudes towards the self can change when one encounters a positive experience with people and life.

The cure for
low self-esteem?

Parents who find their child lacking in self-respect discover if they provide a loving, accepting atmosphere, the child's self-concept will change over a period of time with consistent effort.

However, the longer a child lives with a low opinion of himself, the more difficult becomes the task of dislodging such feelings.

Daily reassurance

Express verbal acceptance
of your child daily.

Always speak positively
about him – especially in
his presence.

Reinforce your child's positive
behaviour by commenting
on it.

Comparisons are odious

Avoid comparing your child with others – brothers, sisters, neighbours' children, friends at school, Dad, relatives, or you when you were his age.

Like your child just the way he is.

Meaningful words

Mention those areas in which he fulfils your hopes and dreams.

One of a child's greatest needs is to hear meaningful words of acceptance for him as a person, not just in the things he does.

Peer rejection

If your child is experiencing rejection
by his peers, encourage him to express
his hurt to you.

Telling him that he shouldn't
feel the way he does would be
a 'feeling stopper' – a denial of
what he is experiencing.

The freer your child feels to express
himself, the more likely you will be
able to discover the real source of the
problem.

The key

Happiness is feeling good about oneself, and the greatest gift you can give your child is a healthy self-respect.

The real place to begin in helping your youngster feel good about himself is with you!

Low self-respect is contagious

You provide a role model for your child, who quickly senses any lack of worth you might demonstrate.

If you have low feelings of worth, they will likely contaminate your offspring like a deadly virus.

What signals are you sending out?

Parents with low self-esteem particularly have a compulsive need to find fault with everything a child does. Soon the child feels that it is impossible to please this parent or to measure up to expectations.

If the child receives additional censure at school from teachers and peers, the blow is even more devastating.

Low self-respect can be hereditary

Low self-respect is often passed from generation to generation in a chain reaction.

Each generation increases the severity of the malady and those who suffer from it.

So break the cycle!

You can make it!

By God's grace it is possible to re-programme a defective self-image.

Scripture substantiates this:
'But all of us . . . reflect like mirrors the glory of the Lord. We are transformed in ever-increasing splendour into his own image, and this is the work of the Lord.'
(2 Corinthians 3:18, JBP.)

A solemn charge

Never underestimate the
daunting nature of your
responsibility.

Everything you do and say is
helping to mould your child.

Children are like wet cement.
Whatever falls on them
makes an impression.
Haim Ginott

Help is there for the asking

Yes, parenthood is a tall order. But you don't have to go it alone.

Divine help is there for the asking.

'I can do all things through Christ who strengthens me.'
Philippians 4:13, NKJV.